IKEBANA (Japanese Flower Arranging)
SIMPLIFIED

By OLIVE SCOFIELD BOWES

STERLING PUBLISHING CO., INC.
NEW YORK

Oak Tree Press Co., Ltd.
Distributed by WARD LOCK, Ltd., London & Sydney

Drawings by Gladys S. Williams

Second Printing, 1971
Copyright © 1969 by
Sterling Publishing Co., Inc.
419 Park Avenue South, New York 10016
British edition published by Oak Tree Press Co., Ltd.
Distributed in Great Britain and the Commonwealth by
Ward Lock, Ltd., 116 Baker Street, London W1
Adapted from "Ikebana New Guidebook"
© 1964 by Shufunotomo Co., Ltd., Tokyo, Japan
Manufactured in the United States of America
All rights reserved
Library of Congress Catalog Card No.: 69–19479
ISBN 0– 8069–5118–4   UK 7061 2236 4
5119–2

Contents

Illus. 1. An assortment of fresh flowers and a few simple tools will do for your first Ikebana arrangement.

Before You Begin

The first step in making any arrangement is to gather a combination of branches and flowers that is pleasing to you. You can use field flowers or buy them from a shop. As a beginner you should select one variety of each, and not attempt to mix different shapes and textures. The flowers should be one color with some slight variation in size. If field flowers, cut stems longer than necessary to allow you to adjust their length later, when you place them in a container.

Next, select a wide, shallow dish or container of a color that relates well to plant material, such as an earthy color. To hold stems in place you will use a pinholder; this can be purchased in a florist or gift shop. It is sometimes referred to as a needle-holder, or in Japan, as a kenzan. A holder which has fine, sharp pins closely spaced is far superior to coarse, dull pins more widely spaced. Anchor this to a *dry* container by placing a small piece of floral clay under it, and, with firm pressure, twisting the pinholder at its desired position until it becomes well adhered and will not pull off.

Going back to your flowers now, use sharp clippers to cut all the stem ends. Remove the foliage at the base of the stems. Condition all your plant material for one half-hour or more in a deep container of tepid water. This will give the newly-cut stems a chance to absorb plenty of water, so that the flowers and branches will keep well in the arrangement. Plant material obtained from florists have already been conditioned in tepid water and may be placed in cool water.

Illus. 2. Chrysanthemums and mountain ash were used to create this arrangement in the class of Ikebana called Moribana.

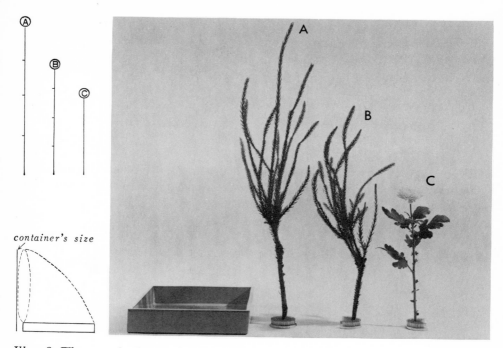

container's size

Illus. 3. These are the three main stems in their proper proportion for Moribana. A shallow dish is used.

Moribana Designs

Arrangements in the category of Ikebana called Moribana are composed of three main stems which will be referred to as A, B and C. Any additional materials used will be called fillers, numbered 1, 2, 3, etc. The A stem is always the main stem—choose the best shaped and strongest looking branch or stem. The length of the A stem will vary, according to the sturdiness or delicacy of the branch, and also according to the nature of the container. Since the plant material and the container are always together, they should be well related in scale, texture, color and pictorial quality.

The size of the A stem should be equal to the width plus the height of the container, or it may measure two or more times the width of the container. The character of the plant material and the nature of the container influence the measurement:

1. The larger the plant, the larger the container.

2. Delicate stems may be cut longer, sturdy ones shorter.

3. A thick-walled container may take a taller design than a thin-walled one.

It is always safer to start with stems a bit too long, as they may be shortened to improve the design. Once cut, of course, it is impossible to replace the piece of stem.

The B stem measurement should be three-fourths the length of A.

The C stem measurement should be three-fourths the length of B.

The Moribana Upright Manner

Illus. 4. Stem A.

Illus. 5. Stem B.

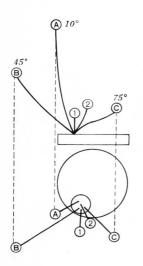

Illus. 6. Stem C.

To create a Moribana arrangement in the upright manner, anchor the pin-holder to the left front of the dish. Place the A stem in a vertical position at the left rear of the holder, leaning it slightly left and forward. Place the B stem

Illus. 7. A completed Moribana in the Upright Manner.

at a sharper angle to the left and front. Place the C stem (a flower) at a sharp angle to the right and front.

To better understand the position of the stems, observe the two accompanying diagrams which show the degree of the angles, as seen from the front and above the arrangement. The two fillers, numbered 1 and 2, are added near the middle to complete the design.

Additional flower leaves (chrysanthemum in this arrangement) are used to cover the pinholder and conceal the bareness at the lowest part of the design. Do *not* make an even ring of foliage around the base. This creates an unnatural effect. Any added foliage should appear to be attached to the flower stems. A small amount of moss or pebbles may be added close to the pinholder to give the design a finished look and a natural appearance.

All plant material needs a constant supply of fresh, cool water to remain in a fresh condition. You must therefore add water to your arrangement. (After being conditioned in tepid water, flowers and foliage should be kept in deep, cool water until they are placed in an arrangement. More will be said about this in a later chapter.) You may fill your container with fresh water after anchoring supports and before you begin to arrange flowers, or the water may be added as soon as the design is completed. This applies to all containers, the dish you used in this arrangement and the vases or pin cups you will be using in later arrangements.

Every Ikebana arrangement can be made in reverse. Naturally, the best side of flowers and branches should face the observer. If your plant material looks best facing the opposite way, it would be advantageous to place the pinholder in the *right* front of the dish and reverse (left to right) the entire procedure for placing the stems.

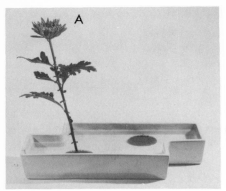

Illus. 8. Stem A.

Illus. 9. Stem B.

A Variation of Moribana Upright

This design differs from the usual Moribana Upright Manner in as much as the plant material is divided between two pinholders instead of being contained in one.

In the diagram the A and B lines are in the front left pinholder and the C line is in the rear right pinholder. The fillers are arranged in the pinholders according to the diagrams. Filler number 6, a small cluster of flowers, is in the left holder, adding variety of size to that group. This is a very pleasing variation and may be created with two or three different kinds of flowers. An attractive combination could be forced springtime branches, such as flowering quince or peach, in combination with small garden flowers. Notice that the stem measurement of this design adheres to the basic one in which A is equal to the width of the dish plus its height.

The unoccupied expanse of water in most Moribana arrangements is an important part of a design, adding a tranquil effect and helping to balance the arrangement.

Illus. 10. Stem C.

*Illus. 11. A finished variation of the Mori-
bana Upright.*

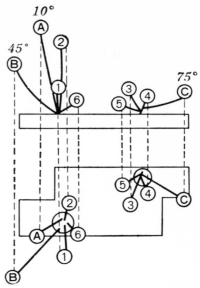

The Moribana Slanting Manner

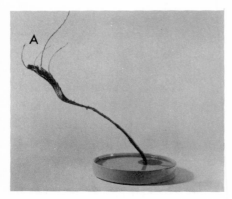

Illus. 12. Stem A.

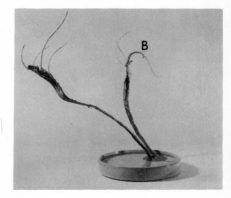

Illus. 13. Stem B.

Illus. 14. Stem C.

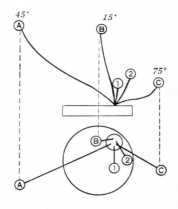

In this style the pinholder is secured at the rear right side of the dish. (An alternate position could be the left front as in the first design.) The A stem inclines forward, while the B stem is at the rear. The C stem (a flower) to the lower right completes the imaginary triangle formed by the ends of the three main lines. This triangular pattern is characteristic of Ikebana. Emphasis is on

14

Illus. 15. A completed Moribana in the Slanting Manner.

the lovely slanting line of A, making this a suitable design when you use naturally curving line material.

Place the A stem at the left front of the pinholder, extending it left and at the same time slanting it forward. Place B stem at the back of A, slanting it slightly to the left. Place C at an angle to the right, also tilting it forward. The two extra flowers, one lower than the other, are simply to add to the design. An additional leaf or two will disguise the pinholder. The two accompanying diagrams illustrate the degree of the angles as seen from the front and above.

Occasionally basic measurements are disregarded in the Slanting Manner. The individual characteristics of the material are allowed to determine the most attractive positions, demonstrating that there is some freedom of expression within Ikebana.

Illus. 16. Stem A.   *Illus. 17. Stem B added.*

The Moribana Cascade Manner

This style of Ikebana is ideal for vines, for materials which twine or suspend, or have great natural flexibility. The individuality and the significance of the Cascade Manner lie in the emphasis on line and movement. To bring out these characteristics to best advantage only a few materials are arranged together. Because the A stem curves downward, choose a container, such as shown here, with a tall stand.

Let A stem curve sharply to front and downward, swinging to the left. Place B stem behind it, to curve in the opposite direction, for balance. Place C stem almost upright behind these two lines, since one is cascading forward and the other is horizontal. No filler is used in this arrangement as the C stem has sufficient leaves attached to it. If a shallow container is used for this design, the arrangement should be placed on a shelf or near the edge of a table to allow room for the A line to cascade.

16

Illus. 18. Addition of Stem C completes this Cascade Moribana.

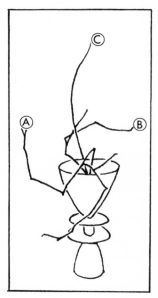

Illus. 19. Stem A.

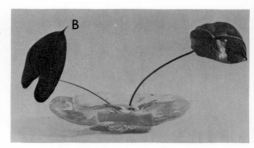

Illus. 20. Stem B.

Illus. 21. Stem C.

The Moribana Horizontal Manner

Plant materials often dictate the manner in which they are best displayed. The beauty of some is brought out by an erect line; some will appear more graceful when placed in a slanting position. Use the Horizontal Manner for material that will be best shown in a low wide-spread arrangement. This is appropriate for a dinner or coffee table.

Using flowers that bloom one to a stem, such as anthurium, place the A stem

Illus. 22. A completed Moribana in the Horizontal Manner.

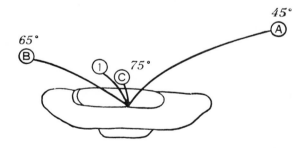

in the holder extending to the right at a sharp angle. Place B to extend to the left in a slightly lower position than A, and toward the front. Place C at the middle of the front, very short-stemmed and slanted downward. The one filler is a leaf placed behind C.

Illus. 23. A four-sided Moribana seen from the front.

The Moribana
Four-Sided Manner

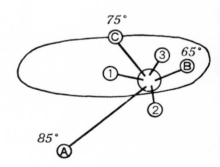

This design is ideal for a table decoration where it will be viewed from all sides. You will note from the accompanying diagram that, as seen from the top, the three foliage lines, A, B and C, form a large triangle, while the three flower fillers, 1, 2 and 3, form a smaller triangle within the larger one. The outline of

Illus. 24. The rear view of the same Moribana arrangement.

the smaller triangle must stay within the larger one. Each foliage branch and each flower or flower cluster faces outward. The result will be an arrangement that is attractive from every side. This is an easy pattern to follow and can be adapted to many kinds of plant material.

Moribana Landscapes

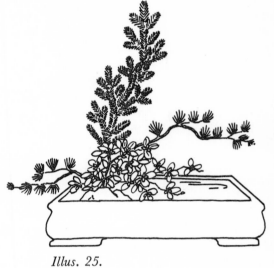

Illus. 25.

One of the most exquisite Moribana designs is the creation of miniature landscapes. This truly Oriental form of art can depict dense mountains and deep valleys, verdant woodlands, swamps and marshes, ponds and reflection pools, craggy seaside views or even the individual beauties associated with each of the four seasons.

The reproduction of natural beauty is bound to tempt you, even if you are a novice arranger, for in this manner you will combine appropriate greens with pieces of rock, moss, grasses or bits of weathered wood to produce a Moribana picture of a remembered or imagined scene.

One rule you should observe is this: allow only one portion of a shallow container to be used for the material; leave the rest as open space to give the illusion of the vastness or serenity usually associated with nature.

A landscape design is based on traditional Moribana lines, using the three main stems, A, B and C. It would be difficult to produce a landscape effect by placing the three main stems in one pinholder; therefore they and any filler material should be divided so they are held by anywhere from two to five pinholders. Keep in mind that the tallest line should be put toward the back with the lower and lesser materials placed forward and to the side.

Individual groupings could represent the islands of Japan, while a pyramidal rock would be reminiscent of Mt. Fuji. A curved or arching piece of wood or stone can indicate a bridge between islands. A series of small flat stones could duplicate the stepping stones used in ponds. Needless to say, any flowers used in a landscape must be quite small, to keep in proper scale with other materials representing taller trees and shrubs.

The finished landscape should produce a three-dimensional picture pleasing to the eye and a delight to the creator.

Traditionally the A line should represent the trees of the mountains or forests, the B line the shrubs on the slopes and lowlands, and the C line the ground plants. Filler material can complement and augment any of these lines to unify the design as a whole.

If you choose to portray a scene picturing one of the four seasons, select material that is naturally compatible with the particular time of year. The ethereal delicacy of spring calls for early foliage colors, small budding branches or young burgeoning blossoms emerging from the earth. Summer would call for warmer, richer hues in full maturity, deeper and brighter greens, and a greater abundance of flowers. Autumn, a truly exciting season, full of moods, evokes an image of bounty and a hint of the culmination of the harvest. It is the time for vivid flaming tones of leaves turned into autumnal glory. Fruiting or berried branches or tall grasses indicate the climax of the growing season. Winter, the season of cold winds, snow, bare branches and starkness gives the arranger an opportunity to bring forth the beauty of a bare branch, a bit of windswept evergreen, exposed barren earth, rocks and moss. Water is omitted from the landscape dish depicting winter, as the ground would naturally be frozen and dry. Substitute moss for water in the dish. However, since plant material must have water, use pin cups (see later chapter) filled with water instead of pinholders for your arrangement. Conceal the pin cups by filling the dish with the moss. The dish may also be left bare and dry, using the moss only to conceal the pin cups.

Collecting and Conditioning Plant Material

Now that you have experimented with various flower arrangements you will want to know more about blossoms and foliage.

The best time to gather plant material is before sunrise, while the next best time is in the evening. A cloudy day is better than a sunny day.

Cut material should be placed in a deep container of water and kept in a dark, cool, draft-free place for an hour or two before you begin your arrangements. Tepid water will cool to the correct temperature in this time. A fine misting of water will maintain the material in a turgid condition.

Preparing Stems:

1. Cut the stem end while it is underwater (illus. 26).

2. Split or crush an inch or two of stem ends on all woody branches (illus. 27 and 28). This allows the material to absorb more water. Woody stems should be split or crushed as soon as they are removed from the tree or shrub and they should then be plunged immediately into deep, tepid water. This procedure applies to evergreen branches, flowering branches, foliage branches and all other material that has a hard-textured stem.

3. Dip stem ends in 2 inches of boiling water if the plant material has a hard exterior and a spongy interior. Protect the rest of the stem, flowers or leaves from the steam. Boil the stem ends for 5 minutes. This forces air into the stem, expanding it. The secret of this procedure is to plunge the stems into cold water immediately after boiling. Now the stems contract and draw up fresh water. Stems may be recut when ready to arrange. This method applies to many garden flowers such as amaranth, gerbera, peony, hydrangea and snapdragon.

Illus. 26.

Illus. 27.

Illus. 28.

4. Burn stem ends on all material that has a milky sap, a juicy stem or branches noted for wilting. Place 1 inch of the stem end over a hot flame until it glows red (illus. 29). Protect the rest of the material from the heat. Burning the stem changes it to charcoal, which is porous and absorbs water easily. While the stem is still glowing plunge it into cold water. Some materials which will need this treatment are aster, bellflower, Christmas rose, dahlia, Oriental poppy, oleander and poinsettia.

5. The salt method is used two ways. If material is difficult to condition, use the boiling water method and add 1 teaspoon of salt to the water. Otherwise, dry salt may be rubbed on the cut ends (illus. 30). The salt helps to preserve the moisture within the stem. Try salt for amaranth, anemone, calla lily, cosmos, Nandina and lilac.

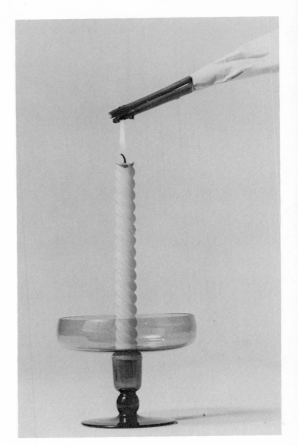

Illus. 29.

6. Sugar may be added to the water for tulips and verbena. The flowers will last much longer, as the sugar supplies carbohydrates to the plant tissues. Add 1 teaspoon of sugar to the container.

7. Alcohol or Japanese sake may be used to keep flowering wisteria or anemones fresh. Place freshly cut stem ends in either one for a half-hour (illus. 31).

Fortunately, most material needs no special treatment. The above suggestions are given to solve special problems and should only be used where necessary.

26

Illus. 30.

Illus. 31.

27

Illus. 32. Use small carnations, not exhibition ones, for traditional Ikebana.

Selection of Plant Material for Ikebana

Nature provides us with an abundance of flowers and branches to use for decoration. The variations of color, form and fragrance are a challenge to the flower arranger. Seasonal changes bring transient beauty to plants.

When you select material for traditional Ikebana, the ideal branches are those with graceful, natural curves. The leaves on branches or the needles on evergreens should be reasonably small or short. The leaf size has to be in good relationship to additional materials and to the container.

Branches that have side twigs arranged in an alternating pattern along the branch are more pleasing than those that have the twigs arranged opposite each other. Keep this important feature in mind when you select line branches.

If you have your own garden, withhold pruning of shrubs and vines until the end of the growing season on subjects that are especially good for arrangements. Wisteria tendrils will assume very interesting, twisting lines. Evergreen shrubs, such as Taxus, when grown without shearing, will supply you with long graceful branches ideal for Ikebana.

Desirable fruiting branches are those that bear small-sized fruits. A good example is crab apple. Graceful flowering branches that carry a sparce amount of blooms are in better scale for an arrangement than overloaded ones.

Small cluster flowers will maintain the Oriental feeling in a traditional design. As an example, the small, refined size of cluster narcissi are more appropriate than the flamboyant size of large trumpet daffodils. Small beardless iris would arrange more satisfactorily than the large, hybrid, bearded iris. Most large flower forms, such as exhibition dahlias or chrysanthemums, hydrangeas or peonies, generally are oversized for traditional arrangements. Use these, instead, for modern designs, where forms can be massive. Small chrysanthemums and carnations are suitable for traditional arrangements. Bear in mind that you are not limited to the plant materials shown in the illustrations.

When you select flowers according to color, there are a few color harmonies that will be helpful. A monochromatic harmony is composed of tints and shades of one color. An analogous harmony is composed of a small group of touching colors on a color wheel. An example is orange, yellow and green, or green, blue and violet. Complementary colors are those opposite each other on a color wheel. Some examples are red and green, blue and orange, or violet and yellow. For a pleasing effect, use a small amount of one color with a larger amount of the other.

The use of red and white in arrangements for many festive Japanese occasions is an interesting symbolism connected with Ikebana.

Illus. 33.

Illus. 34.

Moribana
Working
Techniques

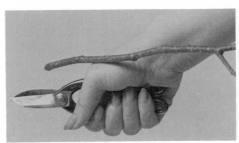

Illus. 35.

On the following pages are some helpful hints on how to cut, trim and secure stems and branches most effectively.

HOW TO CUT BRANCHES OR STEMS:

1. Use sharp scissors, shears or clippers (illus. 33).
2. Make a clean cut at the desired point (illus. 34).
3. Squeeze the cutters with firm pressure (illus. 35).

HOW TO PLACE A BRANCH (branches up to the size of a little finger) ON A PINHOLDER:

1. Cut the end on a slant (illus. 36).
2. First place the branch straight up in the holder (illus. 37).
3. Then slant the branch, having the cut end facing up (illus. 38). If reversed, the branch will not stay in place. The bark is softer than the inner wood and will press into the pins more easily.

Illus. 36.

Illus. 39

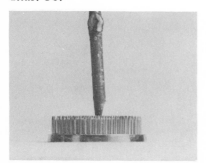

Illus. 37.

Illus. 40.

Illus. 38.

Illus. 41.

HOW TO HANDLE BIG BRANCHES:

1. Cut the end, slanted on both sides. This produces a flat triangle (illus. 39).

2. An extra pinholder is placed upside down on the first holder, to counter-balance the weight of the branch (illus. 40).

3. Place the branch in the holder as shown (illus. 41).

31

Illus. 42.

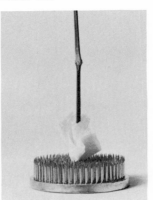

Illus. 43.

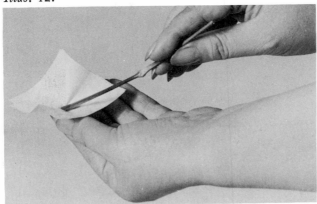

Illus. 44.

Illus. 45.

HOW TO HANDLE THIN BRANCHES:

1. Add an extra piece of stem beside the first one (illus. 42).

2. Bind them together with wire or thread. The double stem will hold securely in the pins (illus. 43).

HOW TO HOLD VERY THIN STEMS (such as sweet peas):

1. Wrap a small square of paper around the end of the stem (illus. 44).

2. Place the wrapped stem in the pinholder (illus. 45).

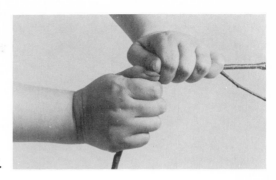

Illus. 46.

Illus. 47.

Illus. 48.

HOW TO BEND MATERIALS:

1. Regular branches—Using both hands, grip with the thumbs and exert pressure on the branch, bending it slowly (illus. 46).

2. Grass—Apply the same technique, twisting the stem a bit (illus. 47).

3. Leaves—Hold the end of the stem. With the other hand gently twist the leaf (illus. 48).

33

Illus. 49.

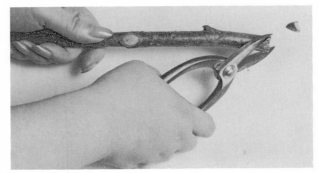

Illus. 50.

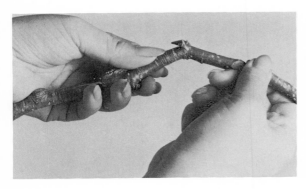

Illus. 51.

4. Big branches—Cut a slant-wise slash at the point where the branch is to be bent (illus. 49). Clip a small triangular wood wedge (illus. 50) and insert it into the slash (illus. 51). Several cuts and wedges may be needed, depending on the degree of the desired curve.

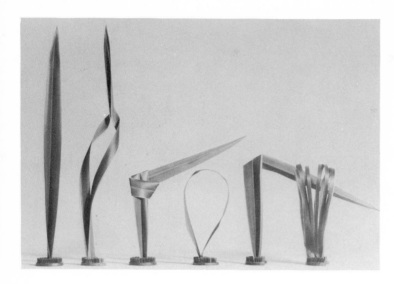

Illus. 52.

DIFFERENT WAYS TO USE LEAVES:

1. Besides twisting the leaf, you can knot it or shred it as shown in illus. 52.
2. Leaves may be cut and reshaped as in illus. 53.

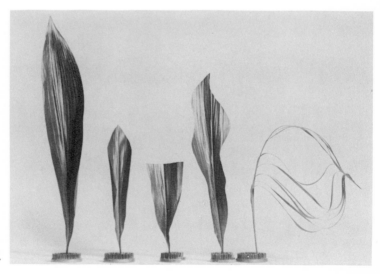

Illus. 53.

Illus. 54.

Illus. 55.

Illus. 56.

Illus. 57.

36

Illus. 58.   *Illus. 59.*

TRIMMING METHODS:

1. A flower spray before trimming (illus. 54).

2. The same stem after several leaves and small side branches have been removed (illus. 55).

3. Fruit branch before trimming (illus. 56).

4. The same branch after many leaves have been removed (illus. 57).

5. A berried vine before trimming (illus. 58).

6. The same vine after many leaves have been removed (illus. 59).

By eliminating excess material the beauty of a stem, vine or branch is revealed. Simplicity of line is important in Ikebana.

Most flowers and foliage are perishable. Their freshness and durability can be extended by proper care and conditioning. If flowers are picked when they are young and freshly opened they will keep longer than flowers that have been in full bloom on the plant for a number of days. If you are unfamiliar with the durability of certain plant materials, a florist will be glad to advise you on this problem. A certain few flowers remain open for one day only and are then finished. Examples are morning glory, daylily and hibiscus. The year-round popularity of chrysanthemums is due to their great durability. If they have an adequate and constant supply of fresh water, chrysanthemums may last 3 weeks or more.

There are other factors involved in maintaining freshness in flowers. Cool temperatures are preferable, about 60 to 65 degrees F. An arrangement will last longer if it is put in a cool place overnight, out of air currents. Arrangements should be kept out of sunshine as excess heat will dehydrate petals and leaves. Dry air is destructive to plant material. Therefore, an arrangement will last longer if it is kept away from an open window, hot air, heat, or air conditioning. A light, misty spray of water, twice daily, will help to maintain moderate humidity.

If practical, cut $\frac{1}{2}$ an inch off all stems daily, and change the water in the container. Certain flowers last longer if kept in deep water, rather than a shallow dish or pin cup. An example is anemone. To revive wilting flowers, providing they are not past their prime, cut the stem ends and place them in warm water until they freshen.

Illus. 60. Nageire designs use tall vases.

Nageire Designs

Besides Moribana, there are three other categories of classic Ikebana. One of them is Nageire. The word "Nageire" means thrown-in. The effect is casual, uncluttered and informal. A tall container is used for this type of arrangement.

The Japanese accomplish their Nageire arrangements by a method long familiar to them. Their technique consists of using pieces of light branch material to support the lines of the design. This is a talent in itself and requires some patience and dexterity.

We shall discuss this interesting style of work procedure because it has proven to be very successful.

For those who would like to achieve a completed Nageire in less time, we will introduce a number of Western short cuts.

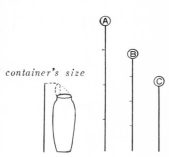

container's size

Illus. 62. Stem measurements for Nageire.

As in Moribana, there are three main stems which again we will refer to as A, B and C. Any additional material will be called fillers, numbered 1 and 2. Rarely are there many fillers in a Nageire design. Again, the A stem is always the best shaped and strongest looking branch or stem.

The A stem measures twice the height of the vase plus the diameter of the opening. The B stem is three-quarters of A, and the C stem is three-quarters of B or one-half of A. These measurements include only the visible portion of the material, and the length of stem resting inside the container must be in addition to the prescribed lengths. If a stem curves sharply, it may appear short in the finished arrangement, but if you have begun with the correct lengths you will be working correctly.

40

The Nageire Upright Manner

This is a basic upright style for a tall vase arrangement. The principal consideration is to achieve a tall, slender design. Only a part of the opening in the vase is to be used for the placement of the stems. The lines rest against the front of the rim.

Place the A stem at the left front, slanting it slightly forward. Place the B stem at approximately the same spot, but at a sharper angle both to the left and to the front. Place the C stem (a flower) to the right, at a sharp forward slant. Fillers 1 and 2 are added near the middle to complete the basic triangle formed by the three main lines. As a guide follow the step-by-step illustrations here and the diagrams on the next page.

Illus. 63. Stem A.   *Illus. 64. Stem B.*   *Illus. 65. Stem C.*

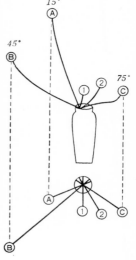

Illus. 66. Completed Nageire Upright.

The Nageire Slanting Manner

Illus. 67. Stem A.

Illus. 68. Stem B.

Illus. 69. Stem C.

This is an ideal style for displaying natural, gracefully curving lines of plant material.

Place the A stem so that it slants forward and to the left, at a moderate angle. Place B in back of the A stem, in a nearly vertical line. Place C (a flower bud) in a relatively horizontal position and to the right. The two open flowers, which are the two fillers, unify the design and add an accent at the middle of the triangle formed by the main lines.

43

15°
Ⓑ

50°
Ⓐ

②
①

90°
Ⓒ

Illus. 70. The completed arrangement shows a Nageire design in the Slanting Manner.

44

The Nageire Cascade Manner

Illus. 71. Stem A.

Select graceful branches for the A and B lines, as they must suspend in natural curves, clearly defined and uncluttered.

Place the A line to the far left of the opening. Use a branch which has a natural curve near the container rather than one which would need force to bend it into a sharp cascading position. Place B, which is an angular line, towards the back of the container, slanting it to the right to counterbalance the A line. Place C (a spray of flowers) on an angle to the left but close to B, and tilted slightly to the back. Standard measurements are not adhered to for a cascade design due to the irregular characteristics of the line material.

Illus. 72. Stem B.

Illus. 73. Stem C.

Illus. 74. The completed Nageire in the Cascade Manner.

Illus. 75.

Illus. 76.

Illus. 77.

The Nageire Horizontal Manner

Main line branches of simple, clean lines are appropriate for this type of Nageire.

Place the A and B lines so they will cross at the vase opening and extend in opposite directions. Firmly fixed main lines provide a good foundation for the rest of the material. Both A and B must slant a bit forward. Place the C line (a flower) so that it is in a central position, slanting sharply forward. The one filler, another flower, arches up and to the left.

Illus. 78.

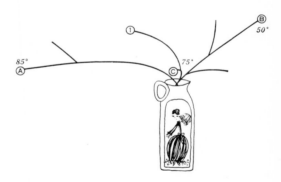

As in Moribana designs, all of these Nageire designs may be constructed in the reverse position if the beauty of the plant material would be displayed to better advantage. In all cases water must be added as soon as the design is completed.

MOON SYMPHONY. *In this arrangement illustrating the Seika style in the informal manner, the harmonious relationship of the orchids with the silver moon container produces a pleasing compatibility. The suspended container is of a traditional Japanese design. While two kinds of orchids are used, the foliage is of a third variety.*

A

BY A POOL-SIDE. This refined Seika design interprets a water and land arrangement. The charm of this design is in the pleasing harmony created by the combination of a water plant and a land flower, arranged as two separate units in the same dish. Basic rules call for the placement of stones, which symbolize land, at the base of the land flowers. The color harmony in the flowers is achieved in the contrast of yellow and violet.

B

OVER THE CLIFF. The unglazed pottery container suggests a rock surface. A rhythmic vine and wispy grass are combined with a charming lily to depict verdant growth clinging to a cliff side. In this delightful example of the Nageire style in the cascade manner, the arrangement has been deliberately placed to the left side and the large form of the lily has been positioned to the right side for good balance.

C

MELANGE. This Gendai-bana style design is of Rikka influence. The combination of numerous flowering and fruiting branches with pine and weathered wood form an interesting medley. In this arrangement the massing of materials is more important than the actual line in the design. The cantilevered wood at the base adds interest plus visible support to the composition, a new approach to a design structure. (Arranged by Sofu Teshigahara.)

D

Nageire Stem Supports — Japanese Methods

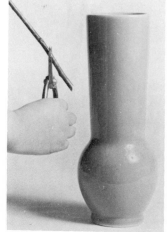

Much of the difficulty in arranging flowers in the Nageire style is in keeping the material at desired angles without a holder.

COMPARATIVELY LIGHT BRANCHES:

1. Cut the end of the stem parallel to the inside surface of the container, keeping the branch at the angle needed for the inclination (illus. 79 and 80).

2. Correct angle of the cut stem if necessary.

Illus. 79.

Illus. 80.

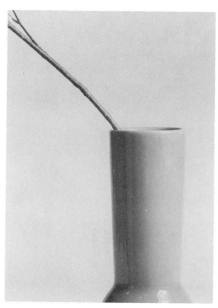

Illus. 81.

Illus. 82.

3. The branch stays stationary because the cut end touches the inner surface of the container, and the branch leans on the rim of the vase (illus. 81, previous page).

BIG BRANCHES:

1. Split the end of branch to hold either a vertical support (illus. 82) or a horizontal side-stick (illus. 84). The length of the side-stick is to fill the space between the inner walls of vase (see page 52), while the vertical support is the same height as the container (illus. 83).

TO BEND STEMS FAR OVER (illus. 86):

1. Press the branch gently but firmly at the mouth of the container, using both hands. Use the first principle explained, or use a support stick, to hold the branch in place.

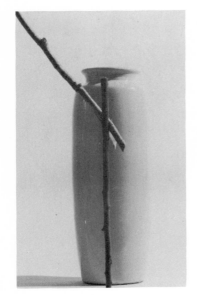

Illus. 83.

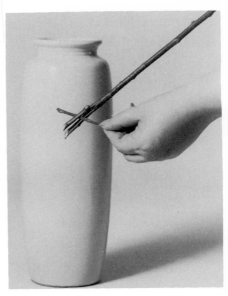

Illus. 84.

Illus. 85. Use methods described to keep branches at the proper angle in the vase.

Illus. 86.

Illus. 87

TO HOLD BRANCHES UPRIGHT:

1. Illus. 87 to 89 show how to insert the branch with the side-stick. After it is put into the vase, the side-stick should be firmly placed with both ends against the inner walls of the container. Illus. 90 shows another method of tying the side-stick to the branch at the bottom. In that case, the length of the side-stick should be the diameter of the inside bottom of the vase.

Illus. 88.

Illus. 89.

52

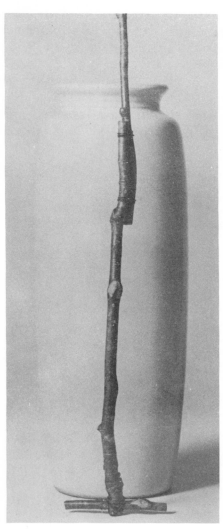

Illus. 90.

Illus. 91. The stem in this vase is held upright by a side-stick.

Illus. 92.

Illus. 93.

Illus. 94.

TO HOLD CURVED BRANCHES:

1. First cut the end of the branch parallel to the inner surface of the container (illus. 92).

2. At the point where it touches the opening of the container, the branch is strongly bent, sometimes even slightly broken (illus. 93).

3. Then insert a support (illus. 94).

4. The branch stays in a desired angle (illus. 95).

54

Illus. 95. With the aid of a vertical support, even a curved branch stays in place.

Illus. 96.

Illus. 97.

OTHER METHODS:
(The following methods should not be employed in a transparent, fragile or irregular-shaped container.)

1. Cut two pieces of side-stick in the necessary lengths (illus. 96).
2. Insert them inside the vase, below the opening, and keep them firmly

Illus. 98.

against the inner walls of the container (illus. 97). Branches of the arrangement rest against the side-sticks (illus. 98).

3. Twisted wire may be placed inside the container (illus. 99). However, it is not commonly used by Japanese artists, since the less support they use, the prouder they are of their work.

4. Light material, like grass, is secured by bending the stem so that the end rests firmly against the inner wall of the vase (illus. 100).

Illus. 99.

Illus. 100.

Nageire Stem Supports — Western Methods

METHOD 1—USE OF PIN CUPS:

Illus. 101 shows several styles of pin cups that are available at florist shops or garden supply stores. A pin cup is a heavy, lead cup in which a pinholder is permanently moulded. It is a commercial item for use in flower arrangement. Some pin cups are perfectly cylindrical. These can be used in vases where the top is flared but the neck is narrow (illus. 102). The pin cup then settles securely below the top of the vase and the mechanics of the arrangement can then be concealed by the addition of small glass chips or pebbles. Other pin cups have a flared shape and these are appropriate for vases with necks that do not vary in width. The rim of the pin cup then settles just above the opening of the vase and the pin cup can be painted an appropriate color for concealment.

Use the type pin cup best suited to the container that you have selected for your Nageire arrangement. To test the fit of the pin cup, hold it in one hand and gently turn the vase upside down over it. This is a safer method than inserting the cup in an upright vase, as it might drop to the bottom and crack the container.

The pins support the plant material and the cup contains water. The capacity, according to size, varies from $\frac{1}{4}$ cup to over 1 cup. Care must be taken when using a small pin cup to see that the water level is maintained. The water loss is not as rapid in larger cups.

A home-made pin cup can be made by attaching a pinholder securely inside a shallow tin can or glass jar. Suitable containers would be a small, tuna fish or meat spread can or a pimiento or caviar jar. They can be made inconspicuous by painting them.

If a pin cup is barely wider than the rim of a vase, it should hold itself at the top without sliding inside. If the cup is smaller than the rim, the vase may be filled with dampened newspaper or sand, leaving space at the top to set the pin cup. Sand, however, makes a container rather heavy.

Illus. 101. Pin cups are available in a variety of sizes and shapes.

Illus. 102.

METHOD 2—USE OF A "LINER" INSIDE THE CONTAINER:

A liner may be a narrow bottle, such as an olive jar, or a liner may be a can or similar cylinder.

Test the fit of the "liner" by the same method used in fitting a pin cup. If the height of the liner is within 2 inches of the rim of the vase, the size is correct. If one liner is not tall enough, use two, one fastened on top of the other by means of floral clay or some cement.

The liner must have a flat top. If it doesn't, invert the jar or the cylinder so the bottom is up. Secure a pinholder (or pin cup) to this flat surface by means of floral clay, twisting firmly to secure it.

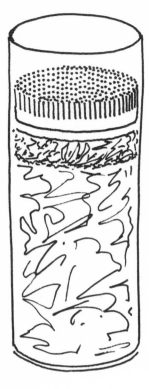

Illus. 103.

Illus. 104.

METHOD 3—USE OF PAPER PACKING AND WAX (illus. 103):

Dampen several sheets of newspaper. Crumple one sheet at a time and pack firmly into container. Add enough paper until it comes to within 3 inches of the container top. (Paper must be damp to make a solid base.)

Follow the paper with a layer of crumpled wax paper, filling the container another inch. Pack this firmly, leaving the top surface as smooth as possible.

Pour melted paraffin wax (or candle wax) over the wax paper surface, a spoonful at a time. Some of the wax will seep down around the wax paper, firming it in place. When a thin layer (about $\frac{1}{4}$ inch) of wax remains on top let it harden.

60

Pour another $\frac{1}{4}$ inch of melted wax and immediately place a suitable size pinholder in it. The top of the pins should be from 1 inch to $1\frac{1}{2}$ inches below the rim. The area above the wax is the only one that will hold water for the plant material.

A container prepared in this fashion is comparatively permanent. However, if you wish to remove the contents, turn the container upside down in a bowl of very hot water. The wax will soften and the holder can be pried out. The paper filler can be removed with tongs.

Always use cold water to clean a container fixed by this method.

The wet newspaper technique may be varied. If you have a pin cup that fits inside the vase, proceed with the wet newspaper, eliminating the wax paper and wax. Instead, pack a crumpled sheet of waxed paper around the pin cup. More wax paper may be needed to hold the pin cup securely in place. This method is a temporary one, and is easily removed.

METHOD 4—USE OF EVERGREEN BRANCHES (illus. 104):

Cut many branches of soft evergreen, such as juniper or arborvitae. These should be cut the same length as the depth of the container. Place the vertical branches upside down into the container. Fill the container quite full, trimming off all pieces just below the rim, so they will not show. Line material and flower stems may be worked through the evergreen pieces, which prove to give good support to firm, light-weight branches and stems.

Evergreen material does not decompose readily in water, so it will keep fresh for several days.

METHOD 5—USE OF OASIS OR A SIMILAR PRODUCT (Quickie and Fill Fast Foam are other names):

Cut chunks of Oasis, a water-absorbent foam block, so that they just fit into the container. It may be necessary to use two or more pieces, one on top of the other, to nearly fill the container. Chips of Oasis may be wedged around the chunks to make a snug fit. Add a slow trickle of water until the Oasis is saturated. This will suffice to keep the plant material fresh.

This method is satisfactory to use for light branches. Heavy material or thick stems will crush the Oasis, causing the arrangement to fall apart. When the arrangement is completed, the Oasis may be disguised by covering with glass chips or pebbles of a suitable color.

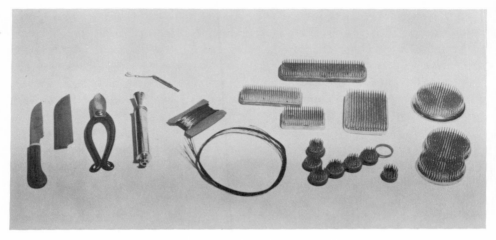

Illus. 105. Equipment, from left to right: gardening saw, scissors, pump for spraying, pinholder straightener, wire for tying stems, various pinholders. To use straightener (below), place it on the bent needle point and bend point upward.

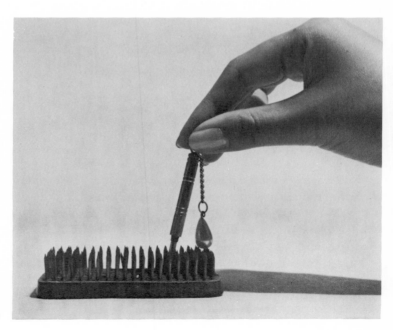

Illus. 106.

METHOD 6—USE OF CHICKEN WIRE:

Select 1- or 2-inch mesh wire, crumple lightly and wedge it down inside your container. Make sure wire is not apparent at opening of vase. This simple mechanical device is inexpensive and easily obtained at a hardware store. Flower stems may be carefully worked through the wire until they are in place. This is an easy method worth trying.

Your finished Nageire arrangement will not reveal whether you have employed one of the traditional Japanese methods for your mechanics or whether you followed one of our Western short cuts. The method that suits you best is the one for you to use. The results will be well worth your efforts.

Illus. 107. Equipment for Seika designs: Background—vases, foreground—pebbles, pin-holder, forked sticks called crutches.

Seika Designs

Seika is the classical style of Ikebana. Chronologically, Seika styles followed the Nageire. Again, the Japanese changed their concept of arrangements from the casual effect of Nageire to the strict formality of Seika designs. This type became so highly popular that a wide range of Seika styles were formulated.

Seika arrangements are governed by exacting rules for placement of line and stem arrangement. In this book we present designs based on three main lines. These are easily duplicated by a beginner.

However, Seika designs are commonly constructed using three, five, seven, nine, etc., lines (always uneven numbers), although three of these lines are still considered the main ones. When a large number of lines are used in a design, it is usually one composed of foliage leaves of one variety, such as aspidistra leaves.

Seika designs are fascinating. There is an infinite variety of containers that have been used for these arrangements. Imaginative pieces range from antique bronze containers of elaborate design to hanging crescents (see color page A), boats and ceramic dishes (see color page B). Many bamboo cylinders are fashioned with two or more openings, one above the other (color page F), as are some of the newer ceramics. If you should browse through old library books on classical Japanese arrangements, you will be impressed by the distinctive containers used for Seika designs.

We offer a choice of four methods for supporting stems in Seika arrangements.

1. Use a forked stick (a crutch) inside medium and tall containers. This is the traditional Japanese equipment.

2. If heavy stems will not balance properly, use a Western prop, and fasten a pinholder beneath the forked stick. Conceal the pinholder with a layer of white sand. The forked stick maintains the appearance of traditional Japanese technique.

3. If you cannot master the use of the forked stick, rely on a pinholder or pin cup inside the container.

4. All low-dish arrangements require a pinholder. The Japanese have accepted its use as standard equipment to anchor stems in a shallow container.

In this book, we present three Seika designs made with a combination of flowers and foliage. The three main lines are referred to as A, B and C. The types of containers used in these designs are correct for the particular styles.

Measure the A stem to extend one and one-half times the height of the container. To emphasize the stature of tall material such as gladioli, the A stem may be three times taller than the container.

The B stem is two-thirds of A.

The C stem is one-third of A.

The Seika Formal Manner (Shin-style)

Illus. 108.

Illus. 109.

Illus. 110.

This style is always slender, barely wider than the width of the container. Reverse the usual procedure by placing the C stem first. Place it at the middle front. Follow this with the A stem filler behind C. Next put the combination A-B stem at the rear. The diagram will guide you. After the material is properly grouped, put in a side-stick over the forked stick to hold stems in place.

One basic rule must be observed in all Seika designs. All stems must be grouped to appear as one, and stems must be bare or plain for a few inches above the rim of the container.

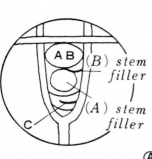

(B) *stem filler*

(A) *stem filler*

Illus. 111.

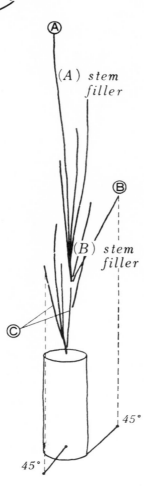

Ⓐ

(A) *stem filler*

Ⓑ

(B) *stem filler*

Ⓒ

45°

45°

Illus. 112. Measurements of stems.

Illus. 113. Stem C and Fillers 1 to 5.

Illus. 114. Stem A and Fillers 6 to 8.

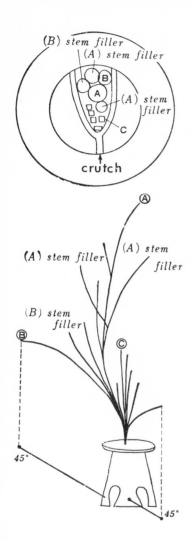

Illus. 115. Finished design includes Stem B and Fillers 9 and 10.

The Seika Semi-Formal Manner (Gyo-style)

There is more freedom in the semi-formal type of design. Lines curve away from the center. Branches may extend beyond the width of the container. There is depth and rhythm in the design.

As in the previous arrangement, follow the illustrations and diagrams for line placement. Insert numbered fillers.

Illus. 116. Stem measurements.

The Seika Informal Manner (So-style)

A pinholder is used in this shallow-dish design. Anchor it in the middle. This differs from Moribana where the holder is to one side. However, the design is assembled like a Moribana arrangement.

Place the A stem in the pinholder at a slight angle. Next, place the B stem to the left, leaning away from A. The C stem is a group of short flowers with their own foliage. Place C to the right front, slanting it a bit to the right. The fillers are pieces of the main line materials. In such a Seika arrangement, where the stems must be bare as they arise from the dish, the pinholder is concealed by placing a group of pebbles around it. As in other Ikebana designs, water must be added.

Illus. 117. Stem A.

Illus. 118. Stem C added to Stem A.

Illus. 119. A completed Informal Seika with the B stem added.

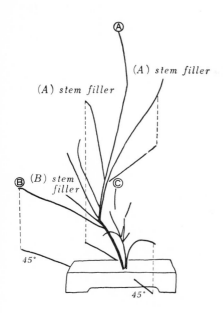

(A) stem filler

(A) stem filler

(B) stem filler

45°

45°

Seika Variations

When using a double-opening container, plant material may be placed in the lower opening only, or a short group of material may be placed in the lower opening and a tall one above. This may be reversed by placing a tall group in the lower opening, extending it high, with a short group at the top. In a two- or three-level container, each opening may have a different variety of material in it. (See color page F.)

A Seika design in a shallow dish may have two groupings, each different, set in separate pinholders, in a similar fashion to Moribana. (See color page B.)

All Seika designs must have stems closely grouped, to appear as one stem. This is the identifying characteristic.

Rikka Designs

Illus. 120. A Rikka Formal arrangement.

Illus. 121. A Rikka Semi-Formal arrangement.

Historically, a Rikka design is the oldest stylized form of Ikebana. Rikka is a tree-shaped pattern of 7 or 9 main lines. One is a central branch. The others are upper, middle and lower branches which are arranged around the central branch. The placement is never crowded; instead there should be a feeling of airiness throughout the design. All stems are grouped together at the base, in a bundled effect, and arise vertically from the container.

The Rikka Formal Manner

The traditional container for this type of design is a bronze vase or urn. Use a forest tree branch for the central line (usually an evergreen). Place this line in a vertical position (see illus. 120, page 74). It may be quite tall in proportion to the height of the container. Each successive branch should be a different variety of tree, shrub or flower. Some fillers may be used but the design should not be packed. Maintain open areas between each branch so that the beauty of each will be apparent. Skilful selection of materials and strategic pruning enhance the design. All stems are bundled and tied at the base, or all stems are inserted into a bundle of slender pieces of hollow bamboo fastened together with straw. The bamboo holds the water. You may also use pinholders or pin cups and camouflage them with a ring of bamboo tied together.

The Rikka Semi-Formal Manner

A bronze container or bamboo cylinder is suitable for a semi-formal design. The same main lines are used. In this variation the tall central branch should curve slightly (illus. 121, previous page). In a similar manner the side branches have more fluid lines. The central branch may consist of any type of material, whether tree, shrub or flower. The branch-pattern and stem arrangement are the same for all Rikka designs.

The Rikka Informal Manner

A shallow metal container is appropriate for an informal arrangement. All lines, including the central one, are quite horizontal, and often of a sinuous nature (illus. 122). The informal Rikka style may have been the inspiration,

Illus. 122. A Rikka Informal arrangement.

centuries later, for Moribana designs or perhaps for Bonsai trees, growing in shallow dishes, as there is a similarity of feeling.

At the present time smaller versions of Rikka arrangements are being made for the home. In the newest Ikebana schools modern adaptations of Rikka designs are a challenge to the artist. Some are constructed around massive pieces of weathered wood combined with a variety of plant material, and are placed on a tray or board.

"Driftwood." The originality in this design represents a new concept in flower arrangement. It is a very liberal interpretation of a Moribana design, placing it in a Gendai-bana category. On close inspection you become aware of the infinite patience required to construct such an ingenious line pattern. It is both distinctive and creative, and masterfully assembled. A few flowers and pine-needle clusters are strategically placed for accent. This design could effectively adorn a modern dinner table or low table.

Gendai-bana—Modern Ikebana

Gendai-bana is a modern or avant-garde Ikebana design. The newer schools of Ikebana now present a very fresh interpretation of the former designs and bring a new aspect to the art of arranging.

While these new designs appear to lack any rules, it is essential to have a sound background of design, based on art principles and on mechanical techniques. It is also necessary that the designer have a well exercised imagination.

All traditional rules are abandoned. The triangular pattern is disregarded, as are the three main lines forming the structure of the design. All semblance of the natural growth pattern is gone.

Materials are handled in many unusual ways, often being placed in odd positions. Materials are used in new combinations and may be painted, dyed or bleached. Colors may be harsh or startling in combination. Textures and forms may be unrelated. The general concept of size relationship may be changed.

Designs may be very complex, structural or geometric. Lines may swirl around and around, or criss-cross into an interwoven pattern.

The natural forms of plant materials are drastically changed. Realism gives way to abstraction. Materials may be placed upside down or sideways in a design. Stiff foliage such as sansevieria (which keeps well without water) may be used in any position. Reeds may be bent to form angular lines and geometric patterns. Foliage may be cut, torn, shredded, bent, folded, twisted, spiralled, looped, knotted or stripped. Flowers may be closely grouped, causing them to lose their individual identity.

Any of these techniques should be applied for design purposes only, rather than for random distortion. However, the artist has the privilege of his own discretion.

All former measurements are abandoned. An arrangement can take any shape or size. Larger flowers and leaf forms are used. Needless to say, classic and free-form containers are set aside for more contemporary designs. Many arrangements are made on a board.

Illus. 123. "Triangulation." This Gendai-bana design using reeds is composed of an interplay of angles. Even the container is triangular in shape. This typifies one of the many variations of personal expression used by the masters of modern Ikebana. The repetition of design and material produces a pattern of great depth and of contrived simplicity. The framework of the exciting geometric angles lends a pleasing aspect to the entire arrangement.

Illus. 124. "Motion in Pattern." The modern trend in Ikebana is toward low arrangements suitable for table decorations. The charm of this Gendai-bana design lies in the contrast of light and dark leaves combined with a creative swirl of bamboo roots. A feeling of great motion is achieved through the variation in placement of the leaves and the extended lines.

Illus. 125. "Discord." This striking Gendai-bana is pleasantly discordant in its use of
two distinctively different line directions and two dissimilar types of plant materials. It is
placed symmetrically in an attractive container decorated with a simple geometric design.
The artful manipulation of leaves and branches produces a bold, new concept in modern
Ikebana.

Illus. 126. "Geometric design." Five flowers and five leaves are arranged with a new feeling of freedom. All lines are placed in horizontal or vertical positions with the exception of the tallest leaf. This diagonal leaf lends variation to an otherwise static design. Two deeper hued flowers add depth and variety to the pattern. The stem placement in this design provides individuality. All stems parallel each other. This is a distinct change from traditional arrangements in which lines radiate from the base. The flaring container adds a note of contrast to the geometric lines of this Gendai-bana design.

Extraneous materials, such as wood, plastic and metal are incorporated into designs. The emphasis of Gendai-bana is on originality.

Resulting designs emphasize force, motion and tension, replacing the qualities of tranquility, simplicity and harmony so typical of traditional designs. The artist expresses his inner emotions.

Since there are no set rules governing the construction of modern designs, this field is difficult to teach. The expression and interpretation must come from the designer's own inspiration.

However, good mechanical technique is essential. You must learn to fasten and conceal aqua-pics (illus. 127) or water tubes within a structure to keep flowers fresh if their stems do not reach water. You should devise ways to attach one piece of material to another. Some of the new adhesives are very satisfactory. It may be necessary to use a saw, drill, screwdriver or hammer to prepare a structure or fasten one part to another.

Japanese Gendai-bana parallels American abstract flower arranging. Japanese arrangers, however, often tend to create low-spreading compositions, whereas the Americans generally lean toward extreme height. The two schools do agree in the use of unrelated materials and in the absence of realism. Both are self-expressive and original in concept.

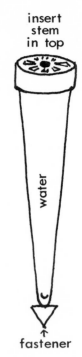

insert
stem
in top

water

fastener

Illus. 127. Aqua-pic.

RICH HARVEST. This design is a present-day adaptation of the ancient Rikka style. It reflects the pattern of a tall, temple decoration, but is scaled down to normal proportions suitable for home use. The Japanese call it a "small-piece Rikka." A pleasing blend of the old and new, this design portrays the joy of a rich and abundant harvest. Many colorful and expressive fruit-bearing branches are used for the main lines, with leaves as fillers.

E

DUPLEX.   This classic bamboo cylinder is divided into two sections, with different plant material placed on each level. The lower unit, leaning to the right, balances the upper unit which leans to the left. Using the same container, it is possible to reverse the placement of the flowers, having the tall material below, and the small unit above it. This Seika design would be equally attractive in either interpretation.

F

FOUNTAIN. A handsomely decorated porcelain vase combines delightfully with the rhythmic materials in this design. Graceful, pendant branches of weeping mulberry are artfully used to symbolize a fountain. The line pattern provides a pleasing frame for the slender pine branches and camellias. Typifying the restraint observed by Japanese artists is the small size of the flowers. The effect is one of quiet reserve, tranquillity and refinement. (Arranged by Houn Ohara.)

G

CONTRAST. *The unusual use of peeled and bleached branches creates a distinctive line pattern. This arrangement belongs in the Gendai-bana style and is a new concept of a Nageire design. The inverted branches characterize a style that is unrealistic but imaginative. Interwoven through the branches are two layers of split and looped leaves, accented by sunflowers. The deep red of the heavy glass vase repeats the color of the flower centers. The rich contrast of line and form is a credit to the technique of the artist.*

H

Ikebana Pottery

At the present time the Japanese potters are creating unique containers that are very appropriate for Gendai-bana arrangements. Many of these are coarse-textured and earth-colored. There are unusual split-level containers, double- and triple-decked pieces, twin-tube containers and free-form ones. Most of these are one-of-a-kind signature pieces bearing the potter's seal.

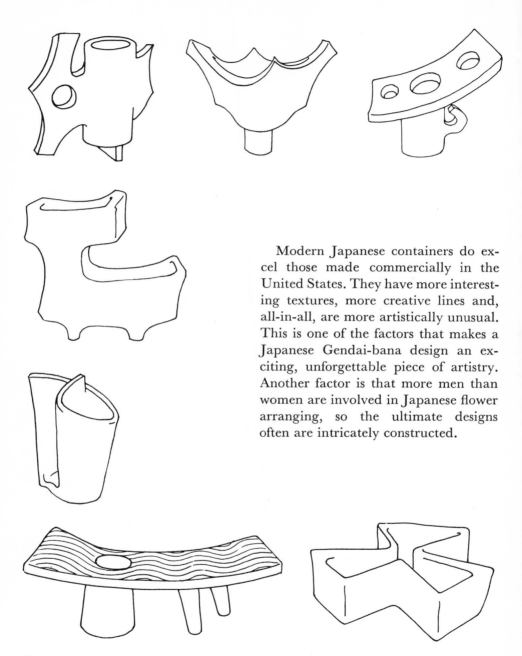

Modern Japanese containers do excel those made commercially in the United States. They have more interesting textures, more creative lines and, all-in-all, are more artistically unusual. This is one of the factors that makes a Japanese Gendai-bana design an exciting, unforgettable piece of artistry. Another factor is that more men than women are involved in Japanese flower arranging, so the ultimate designs often are intricately constructed.

Illus. 128. Samples of containers for Moribana arrangements.

Illus. 129. Samples of containers for Nageire arrangements.

Illus. 130. A Moribana arrangement with the main stem (a leaf) vertical.

Analyzing Basic Styles and Their Variations

To summarize: the four important traditional styles of Ikebana are Rikka, Nageire, Seika and Moribana.

Rikka, or "standing" style, is a large, highly structural, tree-form arrangement. It was originally used in creating adornment for temples. This style is now used for ceremonial occasions. Smaller versions of Rikka are becoming popular for student practice and for home decoration.

There are three variations within the basic Rikka style.

1. Formal: having a vertical central branch.

2. Semi-formal: central branch is slightly curved and the design is more fluid.

3. Informal: lines curve in a more horizontal direction.

Nageire, the "thrown-in" style followed after Rikka. This exemplifies a complete change in feeling. It is a contrast in size, mood and formality. Nageire style uses a minimum of flowers, casually arranged, and is suitable for even the simplest of homes.

There are four variations within the basic Nageire style. (All of these are informal.)

1. Main stem is in a vertical position.
2. Main stem is in a slanting position.
3. Main stem is in a horizontal position.
4. Main stem is in a cascading position.

Seika or "classical" style followed the informal Nageire style. It was a complete reversal in type. The very elaborate, formal, extremely stylized Seika was especially popular with the more affluent members of Japanese society for the embellishment of their homes.

There are three variations within the Seika style.

1. Formal: no material should extend sideways beyond the width of the container.
2. Semi-formal: material may extend slightly beyond the width of the container.
3. Informal: lines may curve freely and extend horizontally beyond the width of the container.

The Moribana, or "naturalistic," style is one of the most interpretive and vibrant styles of Ikebana. This free-style type of arranging gives you an opportunity to use more creativity, more imagination and more excitement in your design. It also allows for more freedom and more emphasis in color and color harmonies.

There are six main variations within the Moribana style.

1. Main stem is in a vertical position.
2. Main stem is in a slanting position.
3. Main stem is in a horizontal position.
4. Main stem is in a cascading position.
5. Design is created to be viewed from four sides.
6. Design is created to reproduce natural growth pattern as in a landscape.

Style Identification Through Stem Arrangement

The most accurate, and at the same time, the simplest way to identify the four main classic styles of Ikebana is to observe the manner in which the stems emerge from the container.

It is frequently stated that the type of container will classify the style of arrangement, but this can prove to be confusing. Containers are often interchangeable from one style of arrangement to another. You may find a Seika or Moribana design created in similar shallow dishes. Rikka and Seika designs are both correct in bamboo cylinders. A Nageire design and a cascade-style Moribana design may both be created in a similar tall container.

The simple rules for stem arrangement that are listed below will prove to be the safest way to differentiate the Ikebana styles.

Rikka

1. All stems emerge together in a vertical shaft for a few inches above the rim of the container.
2. Stems may be firmly tied with an appropriate hue of thread, wire or straw to force them to stay in the proper pattern.
3. Stems may be inserted individually in a group of short, slender bamboo stalks which are fastened together with straw.

Nageire

1. All stems generally emerge from the container in slanting lines.
2. All stems emerge individually, generally forming a triangle.

Seika

1. All stems are grouped closely together to appear as one.
2. Stems are bare for a few inches above rim of container.
3. Stems usually slant to the left or right, but may also be vertical.
4. Stems may need invisible tying, as in Rikka, to maintain the correct line.

Moribana

1. Plant material duplicates the natural growth pattern.
2. Base of stems are usually concealed by low material such as leaves, small flowers or moss. These are used to disguise a pinholder.

Japanese

Ikebana Schools

At present, there are approximately 5,000 schools in Japan devoted exclusively to the teaching of Ikebana. In each, the headmaster gives his own interpretation of the major basic styles of arrangement. Since the variations are unlimited, it is almost impossible, and certainly confusing, to delve into each teacher's particular theories. However, the basic principles remain the same.

The three outstanding Ikebana schools in Japan are the Ikenobo, the Ohara and the Sogetsu. Of these, the Ikenobo was the first established. Started in a Kyoto temple by a Buddhist priest, it has been carried on by about 45 generations of direct-line descendants. It still flourishes in its original location and specializes in classic styles of flower arranging.

The Ohara school, started by Unshin Ohara in the 19th century, is responsible for originating the colorful Moribana style. This school has gradually leaned toward a free-style avant-garde type of arranging. The present-day, third generation headmaster, Mr. Houn Ohara (some of whose arrangements illustrate this book), is a popular advocate of imaginative interpretation of the accepted styles of Ikebana.

The Sogetsu school, founded recently by Mr. Sofu Teshigahara, the present headmaster, follows the general trend popular in art today. It strives for the ultimate in beauty through the combination of nature and art. The characteristics of this school are color variations and unusual handling of materials.

The latter two schools do not practice Rikka and Seika styles, but use them only in theory.

Flower shows in the Western world have recently revised their rules regarding Japanese designs. Instead of requiring an arranger to follow a specific Ikebana school, the schedule calls for arrangements "with Oriental influence" or "in the Japanese manner." This eliminates confusion, and gives exhibitors full opportunity to express themselves without being confined to fixed rules and 5,000 variations on a single theme. It also makes for fairer judging.

If this book has inspired you to enter your arrangements in exhibitions, it will have more than fulfilled its purpose.

About the Author

Olive Scofield Bowes is a nationally accredited flower show judge. A life member of the Federated Garden Clubs of New York State, she has been an instructor for all the flower arrangement workshops sponsored in the Ninth District. Guest instructor for the New York Botanical Garden for ten years, she has for several years taught flower arrangement at the Westchester Workshops at the County Center, White Plains, the city where she resides. She has also lectured to garden clubs throughout the northeastern states.

In 1958 Mrs. Bowes won a competitive award as "The Gardener of the Year" in New York State, and in 1965 was given a National Annual Award and the title of "Flower Arranger of the Year."

Author of numerous magazine articles on flower arrangement, gardening, horticulture and Bonsai, Mrs. Bowes is a graduate of Pratt Institute and has been long active in civic and women's clubs affairs. She is a charter member of the Bonsai Society of Greater New York, a founding member of the American Bonsai Society, and a founder and first president of House Plants Unlimited of Westchester and Connecticut.

In her own greenhouse she keeps tropical and rare plants, orchids and many other exotic specimens. Her acre-size yard is planted with hundreds of azaleas, rhododendrons and novelty evergreens, most of which she propagated herself.

Long an admirer of Japanese culture and art, Mrs. Bowes travelled to Japan in 1967 to study the accomplishments of the Japanese. Her visit heightened her already strong admiration for the Japanese people and their inherent love for gracious living and recognition of the fine arts. Ikebana became a prime interest to her and she became the logical person to adapt Japanese thinking in Ikebana to the Western way of life.

The illustrations in this book were provided by the Japanese women's magazine *Shufunotomo* and represent some of the finest work ever pictured.

Index